W9-CMO-702

A Christmas DRAWING W❄nderland!

by Jennifer M. Besel

illustrated by Lucy Makuc

CAPSTONE PRESS
a capstone imprint

First Facts are published by Capstone Press,
1710 Roe Crest Drive, North Mankato, Minnesota 56003
www.capstonepub.com

Library of Congress Cataloging-in-Publication Data
Besel, Jennifer M.
A Christmas drawing wonderland! / by Jennifer M. Besel ; illustrated by Lucy Makuc.
pages cm.—(First facts. Holiday sketchbook)
Includes bibliographical references and index.
Summary: "Step-by-step instructions and sketches show how to draw common
Christmas and winter images and symbols"—Provided by publisher.
ISBN 978-1-4765-3092-5 (library binding)
ISBN 978-1-4765-3423-7 (ebook pdf)
ISBN 978-1-4765-3447-3 (pbk.)
1. Christmas in art—Juvenile literature. 2. Winter in art—Juvenile literature.
3. Drawing—Technique—Juvenile literature. I. Makuc, Lucy. II. Title.
NC825.C49B47 2014
743'.893942663—dc23   2013005601

Editorial Credits
Juliette Peters, designer; Kathy McColley, production specialist

Photo Credits
Capstone Studio: Karon Dubke, 5 (photos); Shutterstock: ratselmeister, design element

Printed in the United States of America in North Mankato, Minnesota.
012014   007940R

Table of Contents

Unwrap the Magic

Reindeer and snowmen
and presents for you.
Christmas is fun,
and learning to draw is too!

Unwrap your talent with the projects in this book. Just follow these tips and the simple steps on each page. You'll be drawing Christmas in no time.

TIP 1 **Draw lightly.** You'll need to erase some lines as you go, so draw them light.

TIP 2 **Add details.** Details are the little things that show your Christmas spirit, such as snowflakes or rosy cheeks.

TIP 3 **Color your drawings.** Color can make a great drawing magical!

You won't need tape and paper to wrap up these drawings. But you will need some supplies.

drawing paper

pencil

eraser

colored pencils or markers

pencil sharpener

Sharpen your pencils, and get ready to draw all the sights of Christmas. It will be a wonderland of fun!

Deck the Halls

Ornaments dangle from Christmas trees. Draw decorations of your own. Then add details to make them exactly how you want.

Final

6

1 Draw a circle. Draw a small square above the circle. Draw a half circle just above the square. Repeat to create a second ornament.

2 Draw stars all over one circle. Then draw small circles in groups of two or three on the other. Add detail lines to the squares and half circles.

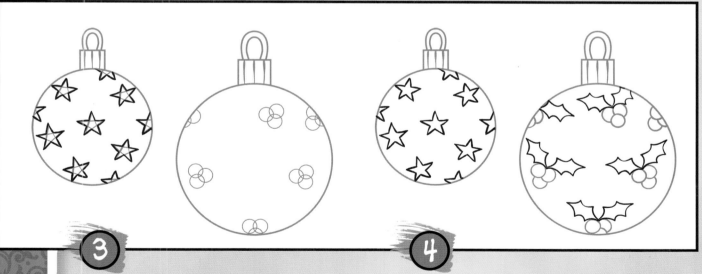

3 Trace over the outside lines of each star. Erase any lines that go outside the circles.

4 Erase the inside lines of each star. Draw two leaf shapes by each group of circles to make holly.

Candy Canes

Make this the sweetest Christmas ever.
Draw some candy canes wrapped with ribbon.

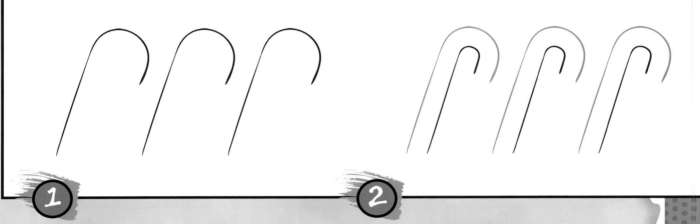

1 Draw three upside-down "J" shapes side by side.

2 Draw a smaller upside-down "J" below each of the first ones.

3 Use curved lines to connect the top and bottom of each cane. Draw swooping rectangles across the canes. Make sure the rectangles overlap in the middle.

Don't Forget!
Erase lines that go under something else. For example, erase the lines inside the center ribbon in step 3.

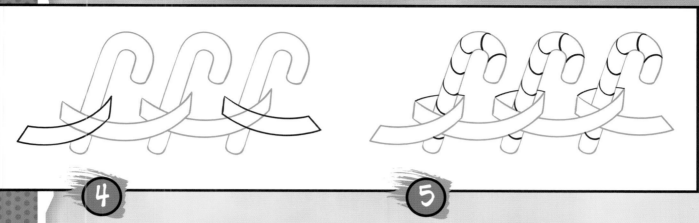

4

Draw two more swooping rectangles that overlap the first two.

5

Draw a curved line behind each cane to connect the ribbons. Add detail lines to the candy canes.

Final

Christmas Tree

Many people decorate their homes with Christmas trees. Decorate your paper with one, and your star will shine bright!

Final

1

Draw a triangle with rounded sides. Add curved lines inside the triangle. Then draw a small trunk at the bottom.

2

Draw a star at the top of the tree. Then draw a diagonal line from the left side of the top curved line to the edge of the one below it. Repeat adding diagonal lines down the tree on both sides. These lines will give the tree layers.

3

Draw scalloped lines just above each curved line. Trace over the outside lines of the star. Then erase the middle lines of the star.

4

Add short double lines to connect the star to the tree. Draw curved lines down the tree to look like ribbon. Add circles in different sizes for ornaments.

No-Melt Man

It doesn't matter what the temperature is outside. Draw this snowman to have a friend that will never melt away.

Final

1

Draw a large circle. Then draw a smaller circle overlapping the first. Add a curved line across the top circle.

2

Turn the top curved line into an oval. Add a carrot nose and the start of two arms. Use curved lines to start a scarf too.

3

Use curved lines to draw the top of the hat. Add rounded stick fingers to the arms. Then use curved lines to complete the scarf.

4

Add detail lines to the hat, arms, and nose. Give the snowman eyes and a mouth. Draw two buttons on his belly. Finish by adding detail lines to the scarf.

Skating Fun

Winter brings cold weather. But don't let that stop the fun. Draw a funny penguin playing on the ice.

Final

1

Draw an oval with one pointed end. Draw curved lines where the arms and legs should be.

2

Draw a smaller oval inside the first. Then draw half ovals as feet. Round out the arms. Add detail and scalloped lines to the head to make a hat.

3

Give the penguin eyes. Draw curved lines to start the beak and add detail above the eyes. Use curved lines to round out the sides of the hat. Draw a small line above each foot to finish the legs. Then draw curved and straight lines to add skates.

4

Use curved lines and dots to finish the beak. Then draw lines to round out the skates.

Oh, Dear!

Draw your own red-nosed reindeer.
He'll shine the way to Christmas morning.

Final

1 Draw an oval. Add a large "U" shape over the top of the oval. Draw a smaller "U" inside the first. Then add neck lines below the oval.

2 Turn the "U" shapes into antlers by drawing curved lines around them. Then add detail lines to the oval head and the neck.

3 Draw leaf shapes for ears on both sides of the head. Use scalloped lines to add some hair. Give the reindeer a nose. Then add detail lines to the collar to make it look 3-D.

4 Add detail lines to the ears. Give the reindeer eyes, eyebrows, and a mouth. Finally, add two bells to its collar.

Stocking Stuffer

Fill someone's stocking with something fluffy
this Christmas. Draw a bunny peeking out. Your gift
will make everyone hop for joy.

Final

1 Draw an oval. Draw a sock shape off the edges of the oval. Add a detail line inside the sock just below the oval. Then draw two small circles overlapping the bottom of the oval.

2 Use scalloped lines to make the small circles, the bottom of the oval, and the top of the sock look furry. Add scalloped lines at the top of the oval as hair. Then draw straight lines to start ears.

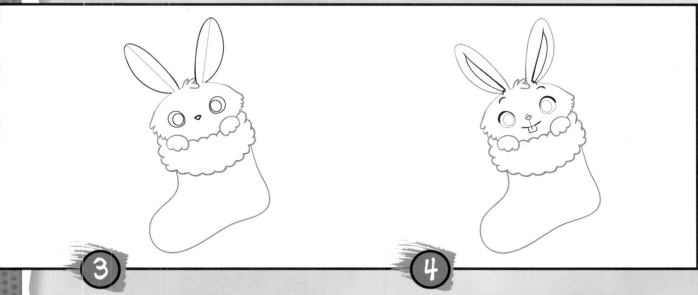

3 Draw long ovals around the straight lines. Draw small circles as eyes. Draw smaller circles inside the first for pupils. Then add a tiny triangle nose.

4 Add detail lines to the ears and eyes. Draw small eyebrows. Then give the bunny a small, curved mouth and a rectangle tooth.

Secret Helper

Elves are Santa's little helpers.
Draw one of these funny friends
to celebrate the season.

Final

1 Draw a rectangle to start the body. Then draw a large leaf shape above the body. Add rounded arms on each side and curved lines for feet at the bottom.

2 Draw a scalloped circle at the tip of the head. Add detail lines to make a hat. Use curved lines to draw hair and round out the feet. Add detail lines to make pants. Then draw mitten hands.

3 Draw scalloped lines to make the bottom of the hat look fluffy. Use jagged lines to add details to the sleeves, sides of the shirt, and collar. Draw a small rectangle on his belly. Draw another rectangle inside to make a buckle. Draw small ovals and curved lines on the feet to make shoes.

4 Give your elf pointy ears, eyes, eyebrows, a nose, and a mouth. Add detail lines to the sleeves, belt, and socks. Then draw two buttons on the shirt.

Home Sweet Home

Real gingerbread houses are fun to build.
But drawing them is even better. Just follow
the steps, and nothing will fall down.

Final

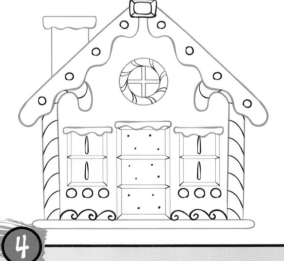

1 Draw a triangle. Draw a rectangle overlapping the triangle. Draw a long, thin rectangle below the first. Add a small square at the top of the triangle. Then draw rectangles for a chimney.

2 Draw scalloped lines on the chimney top and along the roof to look like snow. Draw a circle window near the top. Add rectangle windows and a door too.

3 Draw candy canes along the right and left sides of the house. Draw scalloped lines along the tops of the rectangle windows and door. Add detail lines to the door and windows too.

4 Add small circles and lines to decorate the house. Draw swirled lines along the bottom of the house. Add detail lines to make stripes on the candy canes and circle window.

Read More

Besel, Jennifer M. *A Valentine's Day Drawing Treat!* Holiday Sketchbook. North Mankato, Minn.: Capstone Press, 2014.

Court, Rob. *How to Draw Christmas Things.* Doodle Books. Chanhassen, Minn.: Child's World, 2007.

Keogh, Josie. *Christmas.* Happy Holidays! New York: PowerKids Press, 2013.

Internet Sites

FactHound offers a safe, fun way to find Internet sites related to this book. All of the sites on FactHound have been researched by our staff.

Here's all you do:

Visit *www.facthound.com*

Type in this code: 9781476530925

 **Super-cool stuff!** Check out projects, games and lots more at **www.capstonekids.com**